CHECK YOUR
VOCABULARY FOR
COMPUTING

a workbook for users

by David R

PETER COLLIN PUBLISHING

GW00707535

First published in Great Britain 1995
reprinted 1997
by Peter Collin Publishing Ltd
1 Cambridge Road, Teddington, Middlesex, UK
© Peter Collin Publishing Ltd 1995

British Library Cataloguing in Publication Data

A Catalogue record for this book is available from the British Library

ISBN 0-948549-58-0

Text computer typeset by PCP Ltd
Printed by Latimer Trend, UK

TITLES IN THE SERIES

Check your:

Vocabulary for Banking & Finance	0-948549-96-3
Vocabulary for Business	0-948549-72-6
Vocabulary for Computing	0-948549-58-0
Vocabulary for Colloquial English	0-948549-97-1
Vocabulary for Hotels, Tourism, Catering	0-948549-75-0
Vocabulary for Law	0-948549-62-9
Vocabulary for Medicine	0-948549-59-9

Specialist English Dictionaries:

Dictionary of Accounting	0-948549-27-0
Dictionary of Agriculture, 2nd ed	0-948549-78-5
Dictionary of American Business	0-948549-11-4
Dictionary of Automobile Engineering	0-948549-66-1
Dictionary of Banking & Finance	0-948549-12-2
Dictionary of Business, 2nd ed	0-948549-51-3
Dictionary of Computing, 2nd ed	0-948549-44-0
Dictionary of Ecology & Environment, 3rd	0-948549-74-2
Dictionary of Government & Politics 2nd ed	0-948549-89-0
Dictionary of Hotels, Tourism, Catering	0-948549-40-8
Dictionary of Human Resources, 2nd ed	0-948549-79-3
Dictionary of Information Technology, 2nd	0-948549-88-2
Dictionary of Law, 2nd ed	0-948549-33-5
Dictionary of Library & Information	0-948549-68-8
Dictionary of Marketing, 2nd ed	0-948549-73-4
Dictionary of Medicine, 2nd ed	0-948549-36-X
Dictionary of Printing & Publishing	0-948549-09-2
Dictionary of Science & Technology	0-948549-67-X

For sample pages and further information, visit our Web site:
http://www.pcp.co.uk

To order any of our titles, contact your local book shop or order direct from:
Peter Collin Publishing Ltd
1 Cambridge Road, Teddington, Middx, TW11 8DT, UK
tel: 0181 943 3386 fax: 0181 943 1673 email: order@pcp.co.uk

Contents

Introduction 1

Software... 3
Opposites 4
Useful verbs.................................... 5
Word association 1 6
Anagrams 1 7
Two-word expressions 1 8
Pronunciation ~ word stress 9
Operating systems 10
Two-word expressions 2 11
More useful verbs 12
Communications............................ 13
Word association 2 14
Anagrams 2 15
Know your acronyms.................... 16
Word fields 17
Telephone conversations 18
Computer systems 19
Pronunciation ~ present tense.......20
Good advice.................................. 21
Nouns & verbs.............................. 22
Instructions 23
Three-word expressions................24
Pronunciation ~ past tense 25
Memory systems........................... 26
Odd one out 27
This and that 28
Phrasal verbs................................. 29
Slang.. 30
Computer quiz 31
Communicative crossword 1 32
Communicative crossword 2 34
Communicative crossword 3 36
Communicative crossword 4 38
Communicative crossword 5 40
Vocabulary record sheet............... 42

Answers 43

Introduction

THE WORKSHEETS IN this book are based on the Peter Collin Publishing *Dictionary of Computing.* They contain a variety of exercises, all appropriate for students working in the computer industry. They can be used either for self study or in the classroom.

The book is aimed at students with at least an intermediate level of English. However, many people who work in information technology have to read in English on a regular basis. This means that you may find lower level students with the passive vocabulary to handle many of the worksheets.

Specialist vocabulary

Students will sometimes tell you that they have no problem with specialist vocabulary: *I know the English of my job.* It is not a good idea to take this statement at face value. It can often mean that they understand the vocabulary of their job when they read it. But "knowing" vocabulary involves more than simply recognising it.

Sometimes a student understands the meaning of a word when reading or listening, yet finds it difficult to remember when it is needed for speaking or writing.

Students may remember the word, but use it incorrectly. This may be a grammatical problem, such as knowing that 'output' can be used both as a noun and as a verb. Or it may be a question of collocation: the way some words go together and some do not. We can *initiate* a computer system or *turn it on,* but we cannot initiate a toaster.

Then there is the question of the sound of the word. Can the student pronounce it? And does s/he recognise it when s/he hears it pronounced?

For these reasons - memory, use and sound - it is important to give students a chance to practise and play around with specialist vocabulary so that they can learn to use it more confidently and effectively.

In some ways, learning specialist vocabulary is simpler than learning general vocabulary. It is rarely necessary to decide if a word is formal or informal in style. And most specialist terms have one single clearly defined meaning.

© Peter Collin Publishing Ltd
Based on the *Dictionary of Computing, second edition,* ISBN 0-948549-44-0

But I know nothing about computing

You may be worried about trying to deal with terms which you do not know yourself. After all, not many computer programmers teach English for a living. There is a solution. All the vocabulary taught or practised in this book is in the Peter Collin *Dictionary of Computing, second edition,* which gives definitions in simple English. Many of the example sentences and definitions are also taken directly from the dictionary. If you use these worksheets with students who know the computer industry and you make sure you have a copy of the dictionary handy for them to consult, you should have no problems. Do not hesitate to refer students to a dictionary when they ask vocabulary questions: it is good learner training.

Photocopiable materials

All the worksheets can be legally photocopied to use in class, though if you intend to use most of the book with a class you will find it more convenient for them to buy a copy each.

Extensions

Some of the worksheets have 'extensions' - pair work or discussions - based on the language in the main exercise. These worksheets can be set as homework and then followed up in the classroom.

Vocabulary record sheets

Encourage students to note the vocabulary they found useful at the end of each lesson, and to write example sentences showing how words are used and notes about meaning and pronunciation etc. Use photocopies of the 'Vocabulary record sheet', which you will find on page 42.

Communicative crosswords

At the end of the book there are five communicative crosswords. These are pair work exercises. If you have not previously used this type of exercise, a possible procedure is given below.

1. SET UP. Divide the class into A & B groups, with up to four students in each group. Give out photocopies of the crossword, being careful not to mix up the two versions. Give each group a copy of the dictionary. Go through the rules with them and explain the strategies they can use (see below). Point out that some answers may consist of more than one word.

2. PREPARATION. The students discuss the words in their groups, exchanging information about the words they know and checking words they do not know in the dictionary. Circulate, checking that the work is going well and helping with any problems. This is an important stage: some of the vocabulary in the crosswords is quite difficult.

A A	B B
A A	B B

Students work in groups, checking vocabulary

3. ACTIVITY. Put the students in pairs - one from group A and one from group B. The students help each other to complete the crosswords by giving each other clues.

- *What's one down?*
- *It's used to control a computer.*
- *A keyboard?*
- *No, it likes cheese.*
- *A mouse?*
- *Yes, that's right.*

A B	A B
A B	A B

Students work in pairs, co-operating to solve their crosswords

Alternatively, students can work in small groups, each group consisting of two: an A and a B team. Make sure students are aware that the idea is to *help* each other complete the crossword, rather than to produce obscure and difficult clues, and to remind them to tell their partners if the solution is more than one word. Strategies they can use include those listed below.

Strategy	Example
definition:	It means to make a copy of the information on the hard disk
synonym:	It's a synonym for 'copy'
description:	It's small, made of metal with a…
used to:	It's used to control a computer
person who:	It's the person who operates the computer
opposite:	It's the opposite of receive
example:	For example, database, spreadsheet, word processor...
gap fill:	Every morning, the first thing I do is ... the computer
hints:	It likes cheese
rhymes:	Sounds like 'orange'

We hope you and your students enjoy using this collection of exercises.

David Riley

© Peter Collin Publishing Ltd
Based on the *Dictionary of Computing, second edition*, ISBN 0-948549-44-0

Software

THIS EXERCISE PRACTISES basic vocabulary about software. Complete the sentences in each exercise with the words in the box above it. Use each word or expression once. The first one has been done for you.

---

back up - check - cut - data - database - desktop publishing - exit - games - open -
password - paste - print - save - ~~spreadsheet~~ - word processing

---

1. Our accountants use a _spreadsheet_ to control the finances of the company.

2. The sales department keeps the information about our clients in a _____ .

3. We use a _____ program to type letters and faxes.

4. The personnel department uses a _____ program to create a newsletter for the employees.

5. And when my boss isn't looking, I play _____ .

6. You can't _____ that file unless you know the _____ .

7. You can _____ the information out of the spreadsheet and _____ it into the word processor.

8. _____ the file before you _____ the program.

9. Always _____ the spelling before you _____ the document.

10. If you don't _____ regularly you could lose all your _____ .

© Peter Collin Publishing Ltd
Based on the *Dictionary of Computing, second edition* ISBN 0-948549-44-0

Opposites

FIND THE WORDS in list B which are opposite in meaning to the ones in list A. Use them to complete the sentences. For example: *The opposite of turn on is turn off.*

A	B
1. The opposite of add is __*subtract*__	cancel
2. The opposite of authorize is _____	close
3. The opposite of automated is _____	closed
4. The opposite of backward is _____	complicated
5. The opposite of boot up is _____	divide
6. The opposite of character based is _____	duplex
7. The opposite of column is _____	forbid
8. The opposite of confirm is _____	forward
9. The opposite of contiguous is _____	fragmented
10. The opposite of continue is _____	graphical
11. The opposite of delete is _____	interrupt
12. The opposite of flexible is _____	manual
13. The opposite of hardware is _____	multiple
14. The opposite of infinite is _____	portrait
15. The opposite of landscape is _____	proportional
16. The opposite of monospaced is _____	receive
17. The opposite of multiply is _____	restore
18. The opposite of open is _____	rigid
19. The opposite of parallel is _____	row
20. The opposite of physical is _____	serial
21. The opposite of problem is _____	shut down
22. The opposite of simplex is _____	software
23. The opposite of simple is _____	solution
24. The opposite of single is _____	~~subtract~~
25. The opposite of transmit is _____	virtual

Extension. Work with a partner and test each other: *What's the opposite of 'simplex?'*

© Peter Collin Publishing Ltd.
Based on the *Dictionary of Computing, second edition* ISBN 0-948549-44-0

Useful verbs

ON THE LEFT there are examples of ten useful verbs in computing; on the right there are definitions of the verbs. Read the examples and match the verbs (which are in italics) with the definitions. Then write the infinitive forms into the spaces in thedefinitions on the right.

EXAMPLES	DEFINITIONS
1. Two PCs have been *assigned* to outputting the labels.	a) To 'overwrite' is to write data to a location and, in doing so, to destroy any data already contained in that location.
2. The accout results were *dumped* to the back up disk.	b) To 'toggle' is to switch between two states.
3. The spelling checker does not *eliminate* all spelling mistakes.	c) To 'warn' is to say that something dangerous is about to happen, to say that there is a possible danger.
4. Some laser printers are able to *emulate* the more popular office printers.	d) To 'ignore' means not to recognize or not to do what someone says.
5. The prototype disk drive *failed* its first test.	e) To 'dump' is to move data from one device or storage area to another.
6. This command instructs the computer to *ignore* all punctuation.	f) To 'assign' is to give a computer or someone a job.
7. You *launch* the word processor by double clicking on its icon.	g) To 'eliminate' is to remove something completely.
8. The new data input has *overwritten* the old information.	h) To 'emulate' is to copy or behave like something else.
9. The company's products *range* from a cheap lapheld micro to a multistation mainframe.	i) To 'service' is to check or repair or maintain a system.
10. The disk drives were *serviced* yesterday and are working well.	j) To 'fail' is not to do something which should be done; not to work properly.
11. The symbols can be *toggled* on or off the display.	k) To 'range' is to vary or to be different.
12. He *warned* the keyboarders that the system might become overloaded.	l) To 'launch' is to start or run a program.

© Peter Collin Publishing Ltd
Based on the *Dictionary of Computing,, second edition.* ISBN 0-948549-44-0

Word association 1

WHAT WORD CAN you find to connect each set of four? Be prepared to explain your choice: there may be more than one possibility.

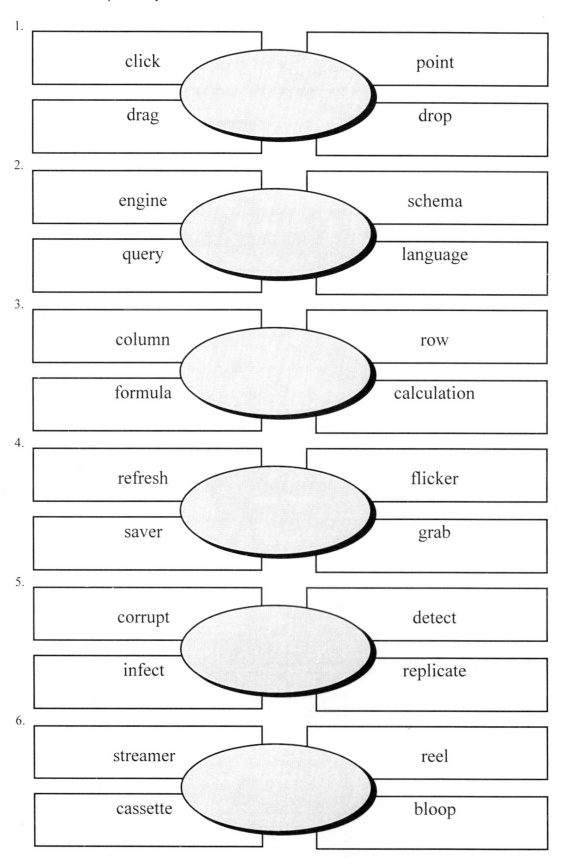

1.
click | point
drag | drop

2.
engine | schema
query | language

3.
column | row
formula | calculation

4.
refresh | flicker
saver | grab

5.
corrupt | detect
infect | replicate

6.
streamer | reel
cassette | bloop

Based on the *Dictionary of Computing, second edition.* ISBN 0-948549-44-0

Anagrams 1

SOLVE THE ANAGRAMS by reading the clues and putting the letters of the words in order. Enter the solutions in the table to find the mystery word.

1. Waiting to be used...ADERY
2. Data in columns and rows ....ABELT
3. Where one system ends and another begins...................ACEEIFNRT
4. Method of organising files stored on disk........................CDEIORRTY
5. System of words or symbols which allows communication.............AAEGGLNU
6. Data which is out of date or which contains errors..........................AABEGGR
7. To carry out, to put something into action ....EEILMMNPT
8. `The user has to ... himself to the system by using a password'.......DEFIINTY
9. With no errors...ACELN
10. Taking place at the same time..AEILMNOSSTUU
11. Separate moving parts or components acting together ....ACEHIMN
12. To modify a system to a customer's requirements ....CEIMOSTUZ
13. Byte made up of five bits ....EINQTTU
14. Cannot be anticipated...ADMNOR
15. Stars, bullets, symbols ....ABDGINST

Based on the *Dictionary of Computing, second edition* ISBN 0-948549-44-0

Two-word expressions 1

MAKE FIFTEEN TWO-WORD expressions connected with information technology by combining words from the two lists: A and B. Then match each expression with the appropriate phrase. Use each word once. The first one has been done for you as an example.

A		B	
artificial		art	
clip		circuit	
desktop		database	
elegant		disk	
expanded		fibre	
hard		friendly	
information		intelligence	
integrated		memory	
neural		multitasking	
operating		network	
optical		~~processing~~	
~~parallel~~		programming	
preemptive		publishing	
relational		system	
user		technology	

1 Several tasks at the same time

....*parallel processing*.................................

2 All active and passive components on one piece of semiconductor

....

3 All items can be interconnected

....

4 QuarkXPress, for example

....

5 Attempt to imitate human intelligence making

....

6 Fine strand of glass or plastic used for the transmission of light signals

....

7 A way of preventing one program using all the processor time

....

8 A language, system or program which is easy to interact with

....

9 Able to store many times more information than a floppy

....

10 Pre-drawn images to incorporate into a presentation

....

11 More than 640Kb

....

12 Simulates how the brain works?

....

13 Controls low-level hardware operations and file management

....

14 Technology of aquiring, storing, processing & distributing information electronically

....

15 Well-structured and using the minimum number of instructions

....

Peter Collin Publishing Ltd
Based on the *Dictionary of Computing, second edition.* ISBN 0-948549-44-0

Pronunciation ~ word stress

ONE OF THE keys to English pronunciation is stress. There are three possible patterns for three-syllable words:

Stress on the first syllable	❶②③	For example: ***per**-ma-nent*
Stress on the second syllable	①❷③	For example: *el-**ec**-tric*
Stress on the third syllable	①②❸	For example: *in-ter-**rupt***

Read these four conversations. Find all three-syllable words and classify them by their pronunciation. Put them in the correct sections of the table on the right. There are 18 examples in total. Which is the most unusual of the three patterns?

Dialogue 1

● Do you know how to operate this word processor?

○ *A little bit. What do you want to know?*

● How do I put a word in italics?

○ *OK. Position the cursor at the beginning of the word...*

Dialogue 2

● *This is my new portable computer.*

○ Very nice. How much memory has it got?

● *Twelve megabytes of RAM and 240 on the hard disk.*

○ How much did it cost you?

Dialogue 3

● *Windows is a graphical user interface.*

○ What does that mean?

● *Well, it's an easy way to interact with your programs...*

○ And how does it work?

Dialogue 4

● *What will change when we introduce the new system?*

○ First, all transactions will be recorded in one place.

● *That sounds more efficient.*

○ And you'll be able to generate statistics any time you want.

Group A: ❶②③

....
....
....
....
....
....
....
....

Group B: ①❷③

....
....
....
....
....
....
....

Group C: ①②❸

....
....
....
....
....
....
....
....

Extension. Practise the dialogues with a partner.

© Peter Collin Publishing Ltd
Based on the *Dictionary of Computing, second edition* ISBN 0-948549-44-0

Operating systems

THIS EXERCISE PRACTISES more useful vocabulary about software. Complete each of the three texts, using the words in the box above it. The first one has been done for you as an example.

Text 1. MS-DOS™

command - default - devices - file handles - run - specify - value

MS-DOS, by _____, allocates space for _____. Five are used by standard _____ and three are reserved for application programs. Very few programs can _____ within this number, so you should increase it by using the FILES= _____. The maximum you can _____ is 255, though using a larger than necessary _____ will waste memory.

Text 2. Windows™ NT

allocated - keyboard input - multi-tasking - protected mode - scheduler
spooling - word processor

Windows NT is an integrated, 32-bit, _____ operating system. Like IBM OS/2™ it offers pre-emptive _____. What this means is that threads are _____ to each application by a _____. For instance, a word processor could have three threads; one to deal with _____, one for spell checking and one _____ documents to the printer.

Text 3. O/S 2 for Windows

address space - crashes - filenames - install - memory - partition
performance

You can _____ this product to run Windows, OS/2 or DOS applications. If you have a large hard disk, try putting Windows on an HPFS* _____. This will give you faster _____. It also means that you'll be able to use long _____. If you have sufficient memory, you can also put each Windows application in its own _____. Then, if one application _____ it will not bring down others with it.

High Performance Filing System

Peter Collin Publishing Ltd
Based on the *Dictionary of Computing, second edition*   ISBN 0-948549-44-0

Two-word expressions 2

MAKE FIFTEEN TWO-WORD expressions connected with information technology by combining words from the two lists: A and B. Then match each expression with the appropriate phrase. Use each word once. The first one has been done for you as an example.

A		B	
baud		analysis	
catastrohic		bus	
clean		~~code~~	
device		degradation	
flip		detector	
floppy		directory	
graceful		disk	
interactive		driver	
laser		error	
local		flop	
~~machine~~		machine	
root		printer	
speech		rate	
systems		recognition	
virus		video	

1 Ones and zeros

....*machine code*..

2 It's one or the other

....

3 A secondary storage device

....

4 It contains only the minimum ROM-based code to boot the system from disk QuarkXPress, for example

....

5 What you need if you want to talk to your computer

....

6 C:\

....

7 Looking at processes to see if they could be carried out more efficiently by computer

....

8 Utility which checks executable files for infection

....

9 High resolution output device

....

10 The fastest link between a device and the processor

....

11 Computer + image

....

12 Allowing some parts of the system to continue working after others have broken down

....

13 It causes the program to crash

....

14 The higher it is the cheaper your phone bill

....

15 Routine used to interface and manage a peripheral

....

Peter Collin Publishing Ltd
Based on the *Dictionary of Computing, second edition* ISBN 0-948549-44-0

More useful verbs

ON THE LEFT there are examples of ten useful verbs in computing; on the right there are definitions of the verbs. Read the examples and match the verbs (which are in italics) with the definitions. Then write the infinitive forms into the spaces in the definitions on the right. The first one has been done for you as an example.

EXAMPLES	DEFINITIONS
1. The systems manager *blocked* his request for more CPU time.	a) To " _input_ " data is to transfer data or information from outside a computer to its main memory
2. He *broadcast* the latest news over the WAN.	b) To " _____ " is to organize.
3. Leave it to the DP manager - he'll *deal with it*.	c) To " _____ " is to distribute information over a wide area or audience.
4. If you want to hold so much data you will have to *expand* the disk capacity.	d) To " _____ " is to stop something taking place.
5. The contract *forbids* sale of goods to the USA.	e) To " _____ " is to receive data from one point and then to retransmit it to another point.
6. Sometimes a program can *grab* all the available memory even if it is not going to use it.	f) To " _____ " is to stop something taking place.
7. The headings are *highlighted* in bold.	g) To " _____ " is to convert data into a form which can be read by a particular computer system.
8. The data was *input* via a modem.	h) To " _____ " is to make larger.
9. The machine *monitors* each signal as it is sent out.	i) To " _____ " is to say that somthing must not be done.
10. All the new data has been *normalized* to ten decimal places.	j) To " _____ " is to look after or supervise a process to make sure it is operating correctly.
11. The computer *rejects* all incoming data from incompatible sources.	k) To " _____ " is to make part of a text stand out from the rest.
12. All messages are *relayed* through this small micro.	l) To " _____ " is to take something and hold it.

Peter Collin Publishing Ltd
Based on the *Dictionary of Computing second edition* ISBN 0-948549-44-0

Communications

ALL THE VOCABULARY in this worksheet is about "comms": PC communications. Complete the sentences using the words in the box. Use each word once. The first one has been done for you as an example.

> *call - compatible - compressed - configured - devices - download - errors -*
> *logged - mail - ~~modem~~ - outputs - packets - password - ~~ports~~ - printer -*
> *protocol - rate - sysop - throughput*

1. The ___*modem*___ connects to one of the serial, or COM, ___*ports*___ in your computer.

2. If the system is not _____ correctly it may halt, or you may find there are data _____.

3. Hayes is recognized as the industry standard, and most _____ are Hayes _____.

4. Data is split into _____ before it is sent down the line using a specific _____, such as Zmodem.

5. When you are _____ to the system you will need to give a name and a _____ to enter.

6. Once you are _____ on to a BBS you can chat with other users or send and receive mail and data.

7. If you have a modem with a low data _____ e.g. 2400bps, it can take several hours to _____ moderately large files.

8. The _____ (the person who runs the BBS) will generally store files in a _____ format.

9. Fax software _____ documents to a modem instead of to a printer.

10. An 80 second local _____ at _____ rate will cost about 4.2 pence.

Extension: discussion. What changes do you think PC communications are causing? What changes do you expect in the future?

Peter Collin Publishing Ltd
Based on the *Dictionary of Computing, second edition*. ISBN 0-948549-44-0

Word association 2

WHAT WORD CAN you find to connect each set of four? Be prepared to explain your choice: there may be more than one possibility.

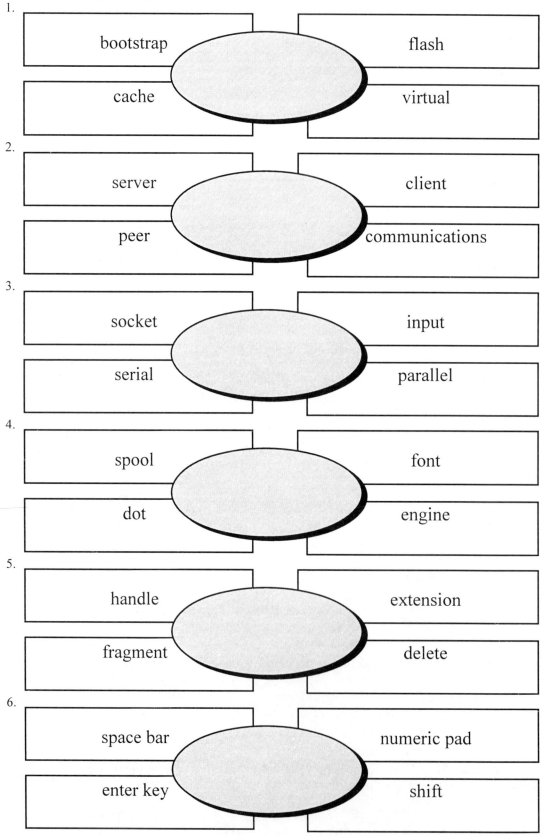

1.
bootstrap — flash
cache — virtual

2.
server — client
peer — communications

3.
socket — input
serial — parallel

4.
spool — font
dot — engine

5.
handle — extension
fragment — delete

6.
space bar — numeric pad
enter key — shift

Extension: Think of at least two more words for each group

Based on the *Dictionary of Computing, second edition.* ISBN 0-948549-44-0

Anagrams 2

SOLVE THE ANAGRAMS by reading the clues and putting the letters of the words in order. Enter the solutions in the table to find the mystery clue.

1. Machine that stores and processes data..CEMOPRTU
2. To copy...ACEEILPRT
3. Scientific investigation...ACEEHRRS
4. To keep within a limit ....CEIRRSTT
5. Fall, reduction...ACDEEERS
6. To copy..AEILMSTU
7. Always in the system..DEEINRST
8. To keep in good working order ....AAIMNNT
9. Unexplained fault in a system ....EGILMNR
10. Symbol of multiplication...AEIKRSST
11. Used to enter information into a computer ....ABDEKORY
12. Measure of the strength of a signal ....EIINNSTTY
13. Sector on a hard disk used to store a file or part of a file ....CELRSTU
14. Loss or distortion of a signal ....ABEKPRU
15. To copy...AEELMTU

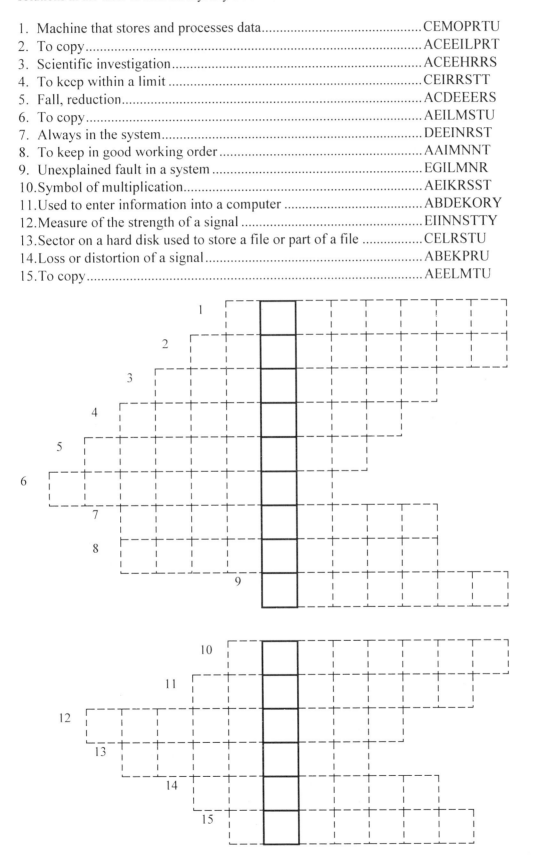

Peter Collin Publishing Ltd
Based on the *Dictionary of Computing, second edition.* ISBN 0-948549-44-0

Know your acronyms

THEY SAY THAT anyone who works in computers needs a good knowledge of TLAs (Three Letter Acronyms). Do you know what these acronyms stand for? Some are easy, some are more difficult. Write the full expressions on the right.

1. BBS _____

2. BIOS _____

3. BPS _____

4. CAD _____

5. DP _____

6. DPI _____

7. FAT _____

8. HMA _____

9. IKBS _____

10. ISA _____

11. IT _____

12. LAN _____

13. LCD _____

14. MIPS _____

15. OCR _____

16. OS _____

17. PDA _____

18. QBE _____

19. RISC _____

20. TSR _____

21. WAN _____

22. WIMP _____

23. WORM _____

24. WP _____

25. WYSIWYG _____

Extension 1. Work with a partner. Test each other on the acronyms in the exercise:
- *What does BBS stand for?*

Extension 2. Write an acronym test and try it on a partner.

Peter Collin Publishing Ltd
Based on the *Dictionary of Computing, second edition.* ISBN 0-948549-44-0

Word fields

THIS DIAGRAM IS a "word field". The key idea - desktop publishing - is in the centre of the wall, and alll the other words are related to it. Match the words in the field to the definitions.

italic   *font*   *kern*

centred   *caps*   *bold face*   *style sheet*

justify   **desktop publishing**   *heading*

ragged   *clip-art*   *header*   *body*

bitmapped graphics | *vector graphics*   *footer*

1. Images whose pixels can be controlled individually..

2. Set of characters all of the same size, style and typeface..

3. Moving characters to the left and right so that lines have straight margins..........................

4. A template which automatically generates the design for a document..................................

5. To adjust the space between pairs of letters..

6. Words at the bottom of each page of a document..

7. A computer drawing system which uses length and direction to plot lines.............................

8. Placed in the centre of a line...

9. Abbreviation for capitals: the large form of letters (A, B, C, D, etc.)...................................

10. Not straight, unjustified..

11. Type of font in which the characters slope to the right...

12. Main section of text in a document..

13. Words at the top of each page of a document..

14. Thicker, darker version of a typeface..

15. Title of a document..

16. Pre-drawn images...

Extension. Create a word field for two (or more) of these key ideas: Databases, Communications, Programming, Windows™ *or* Hardware.

Peter Collin Publishing Ltd
Based on the *Dictionary of Computing. second edition* ISBN 0-948549-44-0

Telephone conversations

THE LINES IN these telephone conversations are in the wrong order. Put each one in the most logical order and then choose a title for it. The first line in each conversation has been marked for you as an example and there are 12 lines in each conversation.

Conversation A. Title...

☐ £240. Would you like to order it now?

☐ Certainly. Which model do you have?

☐ Four megabytes.

☐ Goodbye.

☐ And how much memory have you got at the moment?

☐ No. No, I'd like to think about it. Thank you for the information.

☐ Not at all. Goodbye.

☐ PC Memory Mart. Can I help you?

☐ That sounds alright. How much is it?

☐ The 333S.

☐ There's a six meg module - that's an upgrade to ten.

☐ Yes. Could you give me some information about memory for Zell.

Conversation B. Title...

☐ Do you get an error message when you try?

☐ Goodbye.

☐ I can't boot up the system.

☐ I see. Can you give me your name and number? I'll get a technician to call you.

☐ I'm sorry to hear that. What kind of problem is it?

☐ No - it just goes down a minute or two after starting.

☐ Not at all. Goodbye.

☐ Someone will call you within an hour, Mr Dent.

☐ Thank you.

☐ Viking Computers. Can I help you?

☐ Yes. I'm Arthur Dent, D-E-N-T, and my number's 223 9898.

☐ Yes. I've just bought one of your machines and I've got a problem.

Extension. Practise the conversations with a partner.

Peter Collin Publishing Ltd
Based on the *Dictionary of Computing, second edition*. ISBN 0-948549-44-0

Computer systems

WITH THESE EXERCISES you can practise describing computer systems.

Exercise 1. Label this diagram of a multi-user computer system using the words in the box. Use each word once. The first one has been done for you as an example.

```
application  -  hardware  -  kernel  -  operating system  -  user
```

MULTI-USER COMPUTER SYSTEM

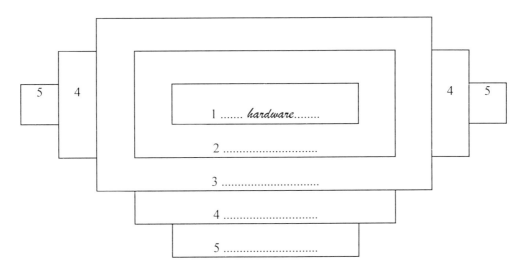

Exercise 2. Complete this description of a multi-user computer system using the words in the box. Use each word once.

```
compilers  -  controls  -  CPU  -  file  -  privileged  -  routines  -  routines  -  selected
```

The hardware is the base of the system - it includes the [1] .... and the memory. The kernel consists of [2] .... which are used by every hardware operation. The operating system is the software which [3] .... most low-level hardware functions, including [4] .... management. Access to the kernel and operating system is restricted to [5] .... users. Applications - for example word-processing software, [6] .... or BASIC - are [7] .... by the individual user.

Extension. Cover the text and explain the system in your own words.

Peter Collin Publishing Ltd
Based on the *Dictionary of Computing, second edition.* ISBN 0-948549-44-0

Pronunciation ~ present tense

VERBS IN THE present tense add an 's' in the third person singular: I work, you work, he/she/it works. But the 's' has three different pronunciations. Look at these examples:

A: /s/, for example *works*
B: /z/, for example *describes*
C: /Iz/, for example *enhances*

Find the third person present tense verbs in these sentences and classify them by their pronunciation. Put them in the correct columns in the table on the right. Be careful: some sentences have more than one example. There are 24 examples in total.

		A: /s/
1.	When he has the time John browses through the Internet and downloads anything that looks interesting.	....
2.	The company designs high specification workstations.	....
3.	I've set up your computer so that it automatically boots up in Windows™.	....
4.	The team programs in several different languages.	....
5.	The software sends and receives mail from within any WP program, and prints it out on your laser printer.	....
6.	This WP program corrects common errors as you type.	**B: /z/** ....
7.	We've changed the configuration so that the computer reads and writes to it more quickly.	....
8.	The program accesses the information on the hard disk and outputs it to the screen.	....
9.	This utility detects and eliminates most viruses.	....
10.	If you buy a modem make sure it conforms to Hayes™ standards.	**C: /Iz/**
11.	Call me on this number if your machine crashes again.	....
12.	When the user installs this program it automatically checks the specifications of the PC and adapts to them.	....
13.	On the first of every month the program updates the list and faxes it to all members of the group.	....
14.	Using this procedure ensures that unauthorised users cannot enter the system.	....

Extension 1. Work with a partner: dictate the sentences to each other.

Extension 2. The same rule applies to plural nouns: /s/ chips, /z/ bugs, /Iz/ devices. Work with a partner and find five examples of each sound.

Peter Collin Publishing Ltd
Based on the *Dictionary of Computing, second edition.* ISBN 0-948549-44-0

Good advice

THESE SENTENCES GIVE advice about what to do in different situations. For example:

> *If you want to learn English, use every opportunity to practise.*

Match the two halves - A and B - to make logical sentences.

PART A	PART B
1 If you want to reduce screen flicker,	• add a maths co-processor.
2 If you want to produce complicated graphics,	• buy a laptop.
3 If you want to store more information,	• buy a laser printer.
4 If you want to speed up your computer,	• fit a faster microprocessor.
5 If you want to do CAD,	• fit a modem.
6 If you want to share information through the company,	• fit a sound card.
7 If you want to reduce the noise level in the office,	• get a bigger hard disk.
8 If you want to send faxes from your PC,	• get a CD-ROM drive.
9 If you want to stop the computer when it hangs,	• get an Apple-Mac™ with a 21″ screen.
10 If you want to import graphics from paper,	• get a scanner.
11 If you want to reduce typing time,	• hit Control, Alt & Delete
12 If you want to make music on your PC,	• make a backup.
13 If you want to do a lot of DTP,	• network the computers.
14 If you want to take work away with you,	• put more memory in the printer.
15 If you want to use interactive software,	• use a non-interlaced monitor.
16 If you want to protect your data,	• use an OCR program.

Extension 1. Work with a partner. Dictate the sentences to each other.

Extension 2. With a partner, write five more sentences giving advice about computers.

Peter Collin Publishing Ltd
Based on the *Dictionary of Computing second edition*   ISBN 0-948549-44-0

Nouns & verbs

REWRITE THE SENTENCES below, changing the verbs (which are in *italics*) to nouns. Don't change the meaning of the sentences, but be prepared to make grammatical changes if necessary. For example:
The two systems **interact** = *There's* **interaction** *between the two systems*

1 The user's new transaction was *recorded* in the database.
  = There's...
  ....
  ....

2 This system is easy to *install*.
  = The...
  ....
  ....

3 This screen *flickers* slightly.
  = There's...
  ....
  ....

4 The new PC will be *launched* in January.
  = The...
  ....
  ....

5 The system *failed* when I booted up this morning.
  = There was..
  ....
  ....

6 The factory is *equipped* for computer controlled production.
  = The factory has...
  ....
  ....

7 A maths co-processor chip *enhances* your system.
  = A maths co-processor is..................................
  ....
  ....

8 You'll have to *compare* the results of the two programs.
  = You'll have to make..
  ....
  ....

9 This is our system for *storing* client records.
  = This is our..
  ....
  ....

10 Only privileged users can *access* this information.
  = Only privileged users have.............................
  ....
  ....

11 It is sometimes possible to *recover* data from a corrupted disk.
  = ...
  ....
  ....

12 The files are *retrieved* automatically.
  = File...
  ....
  ....

13 Jack is responsible for *maintaining* the system.
  = Jack is responsible for....................................
  ....
  ....

14 Something's wrong: the keyboard doesn't *respond*.
  = Something's wrong: there's.............................
  ....
  ....

Peter Collin Publishing Ltd
Based on the *Dictionary of Computing, second edition*. ISBN 0-948549-44-0

Instructions

THE LINES IN these sets of instructions are in the wrong order. Put each set of instructions in the most logical order, and then choose a title for it. The first line in each instruction set has been marked for you and there are six lines in each instruction set.

Instruction Set A: *Title*...

- [ ] Press return.
- [ ] Put a new disk in the drive.
- 1st→ [ ] Turn on the computer using the power switch on the front.
- [ ] Turn on the monitor.
- [ ] Type FORMAT A:
- [ ] Wait until you see the command line symbol C:\.

Instruction Set B: *Title*...

- [ ] Click on FILE in the menu bar and select PRINT from the pull-down menu.
- [ ] Click on OK in the dialogue box.
- [ ] Click on the up arrow in the top right hand corner to maximize the window.
- [ ] Collect your printout from the laser.
- 1st→ [ ] Double-click on the Write™ icon.
- [ ] Type your text.

Instruction Set C: *Title*...

- [ ] Disconnect the printer from the power supply and unplug the parallel interface cable.
- [ ] Open the panel at the back.
- [ ] Push the new memory board in and replace the panel.
- [ ] Reconnect the printer to the PC and to the power supply.
- [ ] Slide the old memory board out of the slot.
- 1st→ [ ] Turn off the computer and printer.

Extension 1. Choose one set of instructions and dictate them to a partner.

Extension 2. Give instructions for a procedure you use at work.

Peter Collin Publishing Ltd
Based on the *Dictionary of Computing, 2nd Ed.* ISBN 0-948549-44-0

Three-word expressions

MAKE TWELVE THREE-WORD expressions connected with information technology by combining words from the three lists - A, B, C - and match each expression with the appropriate phrase. Use each word once. The first one has been done for you.

A	*B*	*C*
bulletin	access	architecture
~~central~~	area	example
dynamic	board	exchange
graphical	by	injury
local	character	interface
near	data	memory
onion	down	menu
optical	letter	network
pull	~~processing~~	quality
query	skin	recognition
random	strain	system
repetitive	user	~~unit~~

1 Control + arithmetic/logic + input/output

..........*central processing unit*...........................

2 Can be avoided by adjusting your chair

....

3 Windows, icons, mouse, pointer

....

4 Allows access to any location in any order

....

5 Sort of database accessed by modem

....

6 "The ... is viewed by clicking on the menu bar at the top of the screen"

....

7 A question to a database

....

8 The terminals are all near to each other

....

9 When one program asks the operating system to create a link with another

....

10 Design of a computer system in layers, according to function or priority

....

11 A process that converts scanned-in text into machine readable code

....

12 Almost as good as a typewriter

....

© Peter Collin Publishing Ltd
Based on the *Dictionary of Computing, second edition.* ISBN 0-948549-44-0

Pronunciation ~ past tense

REGULAR VERBS HAVE three different pronunciations in the past tense (or the past participle). The difference is in the sound you use for the ending. Look at these examples:

/t/, for example *clicked*

/d/, for example *dragged*

/ɪd/, for example *pointed*

Find the past tense verbs in these sentences and classify them by their pronunciation. Put them in the correct columns in the table on the right. Be careful: some sentences have more than one verb. There are 24 examples in total.

1. After the input is received the first function is called up.

2. Everything will be OK once we've introduced the new system.

3. I downloaded all the information I could find on the Internet about this subject.

4. I found the problem when I launched this program.

5. I selected the network laser, printed the document and closed down.

6. I typed the password and opened the file.

7. I warned my boss that there was going to be a problem.

8. Oh no! I've deleted all the client records!

9. The new version of this software was released in July.

10. The printout's fine: I checked it.

11. These machines haven't been serviced for a year.

12. This machine is programmed to find the shortest possible route between sales calls.

13. We dumped all the information onto the hard disk of the server.

14. We moved the DP department to the third floor.

15. We searched the database but your transaction wasn't recorded.

16. We've networked all the machines on the fourth floor.

17. With this system we've eliminated all possibilities of error.

18. You've saved this file in the wrong directory.

A: /t/

B: /d/

C: /ɪd/

Extension. Work with a partner: dictate the sentences to each other.

© Peter Collin Publishing Ltd
Based on the *Dictionary of Computing, second edition.* ISBN 0-948549-44-0

Memory systems

THESE EXERCISES WILL give you practice in using the right vocabulary for describing memory systems.

Exercise 1. Label the diagrams using the words and phrases in the box. Use each word once. The first one has been done for you.

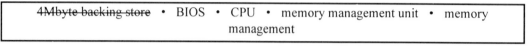

4Mbyte backing store • BIOS • CPU • memory management unit • memory management

VIRTUAL MEMORY SYSTEM

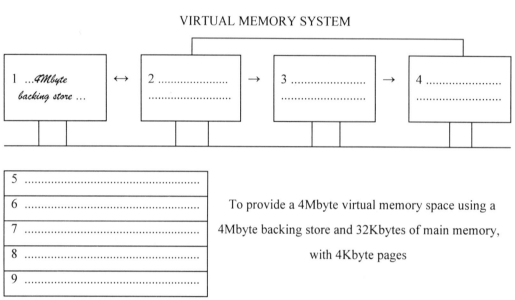

1 ...*4Mbyte backing store* ...   ↔   2 ....   →   3 ....   →   4 ....

| 5 .... |
| 6 .... |
| 7 .... |
| 8 .... |
| 9 .... |

To provide a 4Mbyte virtual memory space using a 4Mbyte backing store and 32Kbytes of main memory, with 4Kbyte pages

Exercise 2. All the vowels (A, E, I, O, U) have been removed from this text and replaced with asterisks (*). Can you read it?

V*rt**l m*m*ry *pp**rs t* *n *ppl*c*t**n j*st l*k* * l*rg* *m**nt *f n*rm*l m**n m*m*ry. *t *s cr**t*d by cr**t*ng s*v*r*l `p*g*s' *f th* *v**l*bl* m**n m*m*ry *n * l*rg*r h*rd d*sk *nd sw*pp*ng b*tw**n th*s* p*g*s *s *nd wh*n th*y *r* *cc*ss*d. *f th* CP* *sks th* m*m*ry m*n*g*m*nt *n*t f*r *n *ddr*ss th*t *s n*t *n th* c*rr*nt p*g* *t l**ks *p th* p*g* wh*ch h*lds th*s *ddr*ss *nd l**ds *t fr*m th* h*rd d*sk b*ck*ng st*r*. *p*r*t*ng syst*ms s*ch *s M*cr*s*ft W*nd*ws pr*v*d* m*r* m*m*ry th*n *s *ct**lly f*tt*d *n th* PC by *mpl*m*nt*ng v*rt**l m*m*ry *nd sw*pp*ng p*g*s t* *nd fr*m th* h*rd d*sk.

Extension. Explain the system in your own words.

Odd one out

IN EACH OF the four sets of words below, one word odd one out: different from the others. Find the word that is different, and circle it. For example:

- monitor..................... printer............................ scanner........................... (spreadsheet...)...............

A spreadsheet is an application; the others are machines.

1	desktop..................	laptop............................	notebook......................	palmtop.......................
2	keyboard................	modem.........................	mouse...........................	trackball......................
3	compact.................	floppy..........................	hard.............................	soft...............................
4	bps.......................	dpi................................	mips.............................	ppm.............................
5	drive.....................	motherboard.................	port..............................	power switch...............
6	local bus................	microprocessor.............	graphics card................	port..............................
7	game.....................	joystick.........................	parallel..........................	serial............................
8	keyboard................	modem.........................	monitor..........................	printer...........................
9	database.................	file................................	spreadsheet...................	word processor............
10	client.....................	peer.............................	server..........................	standalone....................
11	RAM.....................	cache...........................	flash.............................	printout.........................
12	cell.......................	column.........................	row................................	window........................
13	click.....................	italics............................	bold face......................	caps.............................
14	function key............	screen...........................	shift..............................	space bar......................
15	bug.......................	error.............................	howler..........................	message.......................
16	allocate..................	emulate.........................	replicate........................	simulate.......................
17	click.....................	drag.............................	point.............................	type.............................
18	lcd.......................	qbe..............................	tft.................................	vga..............................
19	inkjet....................	laser.............................	plotter...........................	scanner........................
20	beep.....................	bloop............................	wipe.............................	zap..............................

© Peter Collin Publishing Ltd
Based on the *Dictionary of Computing, second edition*. ISBN 0-948549-44-0

This and that

USE THE WORDS in the box to make eleven expressions connected with information technolgy. Then use the expressions to complete the sentences. All the expressions follow the same pattern: A and B. The first one has been done for you as an example.

A	B
bells	click
cut	columns
drag	drop
hyphenation	embedding
point	flutter
rows	justification
search	paste
terminate	replace
tilt	stay resident
object linking	swivel
wow	whistles

1 This is just a basic program - it doesn't have any
bells and whistles..

2 If you change your mind you can use ....
..............to change all the examples in the text.

3 If you want to add a comment to your information in your report you can use ....
..........to get information from the word processor and copy it into the worksheet.

4 The speakers on that PC are very cheap - listen to the amount of ....
they have!

5 You use a mouse to navigate a GUI: you can simply ....
on icons to make most selections.

6 I use a little ....
program to check for viruses.

7 If you ....
the document icon onto the word processor icon, the system will start the program and load the document.

8 An American..
program will not work with British spellings.

9 Information in a spreadsheet is organised in
....

10 Windows uses ....
to share data between applications.

11 We use ....
monitors for ergonomic reasons.

Peter Collin Publishing Ltd
Based on the *Dictionary of Computing, second edition.* ISBN 0-948549-44-0

Phrasal verbs

PHRASAL VERBS ARE made from averb and a preposition. For example:

> *This is the procedure to* **wake up** *the system.*

"Wake up" means to start or initiate. Complete the sentences below by choosing the correct verbs and prepositions from the two boxes. Be careful: sometimes you have to change the form of the verb.

VERBS
back
boot   break   call
log   log   plug   round
shut   turn   turn
warm

PREPOSITIONS
down
down   down   in
off   off   on   on
up   up   up   up
up

1   No wonder it isn't working: you haven't even _____ it _____!

2   You have to give your password in order to _____ _____ to the system.

3   Pushing the big red button on the front _____ the CPU _____.

4   With all the virus detectors we use, it takes me ten minutes to _____ _____ these days.

5   If you don't _____ _____ regularly you could lose data.

6   I _____ _____ all the customers' addresses from the database and checked them on screen.

7   When we found the virus the first thing we did was to _____ _____ the entire system.

8   My computer's _____ _____ again! I need a new machine.

9   Don't forget to _____ everything _____ before you go home.

10   When you've downloaded th information you need, then _____ _____ from the system.

11   Your printout will arrive in a couple of minutes: the laser's still _____ _____.

12   The precise amount is 2.5341, but we can _____ it _____ to 2.5.

Extension. Explain in your own words what each verb means.

© Peter Collin Publishing Ltd
Based on the *Dictionary of Computing, second edition.* ISBN 0-948549-44-0

Slang

IN THE WORLD of computers there is a special slang, just as in any other profession. The ten conversations below each contain an example of computer slang. Find the slang words and match them to the defintions on the right.

i   How's your computer? Is it working now?

It seems alright - it passed the smoke test.

ii   Have you finished with this file?

Yes - go ahead and zap it.

iii   Can you fix this for me?

I'm a bit short of time. I can do a kludge for you and have another look tomorrow.

iv   What's wrong?

I don't know. Some sort of gremlin - the system keeps going down.

v   I'm having problems running Windows™.

I'm not surprised. You need more than a couple of megs to do multitasking.

vi   What did you do before you worked here?

I was a project manager for Big Blue.

vii   They say they're releasing a new version soon.

Don't get excited. They've already made four product announcements. It's just vapourware.

viii   What do you think the problem was?

I don't know, but it seems alright now. It was probably just a glitch.

ix   Are you going to eliminate the bugs in the accounts program?

We'll try, but I don't know if we've got the wetware to do it.

x   What are you working on this week?

I'm doing a comms program to get information from branch offices more easily.

Find the words which mean:

1. Communications

....

2. IBM

....

3. An unexplained fault in a system

....

4. Products which exist in name only

....

5. To wipe off all data currently in the workspace

....

6. Casual test: the machine must be working if no smoke appears when it is switched on

....

7. Megabyte

....

8. A temporary correction

....

9. Any thing which causes a sudden, unexpected failure

....

10. The human brain, applied to writing software

....

© Peter Collin Publishing Ltd
Based on the *Dictionary of Computing, second edition*. 0-948549-44-0

Computer quiz

HOW MUCH DO you know about computers? Can you answer these questions?

1   Exactly how many bytes are there in a megabyte?

....

2   Who invented the digital computer?

....

3   What is the plural of mouse?

....

4   Which company built the first electro-mechanical digital computer?

....

5   What does IBM stand for?

....

6   In which year was Apple Computer Corporation founded?

....

7   What can you discover by using the Turing test?

....

8   Who was Eliza?

....

9   What game can you play with Deep Throat?

....

10   Which is the second biggest computer company in the world?

....

11   Where did the language Pascal get its name from?

....

12   APL is a programming language used for scientific and mathemetical work. What do its initials stand for?

....

Extension. With a partner, write a computer quiz. Write ten questions - and make sure you know the answers to all of them. Then try the quiz on the other students in the class.

© Peter Collin Publishing Ltd
Based on the *Dictionary of Computing, second edition* ISBN 0-948549-44-0

Communicative Crossword 1   Sheet A

THIS CROSSWORD IS not complete: you have only half the words. The other half are on sheet B. Check that you know the words in your crossword. Then work with a partner who has sheet B to complete the two crosswords. Follow these three rules:

1. Speak only in English

2. Don't say the word in the crossword

3. Don't show your crossword to your partner.

> *"What's one across?"*
> → across, ↓ down

The crossword grid contains the following filled letters:

- 1 Down: K E R N E L
- 3 Across: A S Y N C
- 4 Down: S
- 5 Down: C D
- 7 Down: T R O J A N H O R
- 8 Across: H U B
- 9 Down: A P P L I C A T I O N
- 10 Across: E N C L O S E
- 19 Across: O K
- 23 Down: B U N
- 24 Across: T A B L E
- 25 Down: B A U
- 27 Across: B A C K G R O U N D
- 27 Down: B O O
- 28 Down: G R A M
- 30 Across: S L O
- 31 Down: T A B
- 32 Across: T O P
- 33 Across: E

© Peter Collin Publishing Ltd
Based on the Dictionary of Computing, second edition, ISBN 0-948549-44-0

Communicative Crossword 1   Sheet B

THIS CROSSWORD IS not complete: you have only half the words. The other half are on sheet A. Check that you know the words in your crossword. Then work with a partner who has sheet A to complete the two crosswords. Follow these three rules:

1. Speak only in English

2. Don't say the word in the crossword

3. Don't show your crossword to your partner.

> *"What's one across?"*
> → across, ↓ down

¹K	L	²U	D	G	E	■	³	⁴S			⁵
	■	N	■			⁶M	■	C	■		D
	■	L	■	⁷		O	■	⁸H			■
	■	O	■			V	■	E		⁹	■
¹⁰		C		O		E	■	¹¹D	U	M	P
	■	K	■		■	M	■	U	■		
■	■	¹²D	A	T	E	■	■	L	■		
¹³A	■	¹⁴F	■			N	■	¹⁵E	¹⁶M		
¹⁷F	L	A	S	H		T	■	¹⁸R	I	S	C
F	■	S	■	¹⁹		■	²⁰T		S	■	
²¹E	N	T	E	R	■	■	Y	■	■		
C	■	■	²²S	K	I	P	P	■	²³		
²⁴T		²⁵			■	■	E	■			
■	■		■		■	²⁶P		■			
²⁷			²⁸				■	²⁹			
	■		■		■	I	■	³⁰S			³¹
	■		■		■	N	■		■		
³²			■	³³E	X	T	E	N	D	■	

© Peter Collin Publishing Ltd
Based on the Dictionary of Computing, second edition, ISBN 0-948549-44-0

Communicative Crossword 2   Sheet A

THIS CROSSWORD IS not complete: you have only half the words. The other half are on sheet B. Check that you know the words in your crossword. Then work with a partner who has sheet B to complete the two crosswords. Follow these three rules:

1. Speak only in English

2. Don't say the word in the crossword

3. Don't show your crossword to your partner.

> *"What's one across?"*
> → across, ↓ down

A crossword grid with the following filled letters:

- 1 Down: D I S T R I B U T E
- 7 Across: S E M A N T I C S
- Column (2): E M, A T T R E E
- C E, N T R, A D G, A T E (27 Across: N A N D G A T E)
- 4 Down: O X
- 8 Across / 9 Across: A, E N D I N G
- 10 Down: D E F F E T A
- 13 Across: T I F F
- 14 Across: U S A S C I I
- 16 Across: C A S E
- 15 Down: I A A
- 17 E, 18 I E
- 20, 21, 22 S C A N E, 23 R
- 24 E D E
- 25 Down: A P P E N D
- 26
- 28, 29
- 30 Across: T R E E
- 31

© Peter Collin Publishing Ltd
Based on the *Dictionary of Computing, second edition.* ISBN 0-948549-44-0

Communicative Crossword 2 Sheet B

THIS CROSSWORD IS not complete: you have only half the words. The other half are on sheet A. Check that you know the words in your crossword. Then work with a partner who has sheet A to complete the two crosswords. Follow these three rules:

1. Speak only in English

2. Don't say the word in the crossword

3. Don't show your crossword to your partner.

> *"What's one across?"*
> → across, ↓ down

Based on the *Dictionary of Computing, second edition.* ISBN 0-948549-44-0

Communicative Crossword 3   Sheet A

THIS CROSSWORD IS not complete: you have only half the words. The other half are on sheet B. Check that you know the words in your crossword. Then work with a partner who has sheet B to complete the two crosswords. Follow these three rules:

1. Speak only in English

2. Don't say the word in the crossword

3. Don't show your crossword to your partner.

> *"What's one across?"*
> → across, ↓ down

Communicative Crossword 3   Sheet B

THIS CROSSWORD IS not complete: you have only half the words. The other half are on sheet A. Check that you know the words in your crossword. Then work with a partner who has sheet A to complete the two crosswords. Follow these three rules:

1. Speak only in English

2. Don't say the word in the crossword

3. Don't show your crossword to your partner.

> *"What's one across?"*
> → across, ↓ down

¹A	L	²P	H	A	³N	U	⁴M	E	⁵R	I	⁶C
		A			A						
⁷T	U	R	N	⁸O	N						
		T		⁹S	O	C	K	E	T		
		I		S							
¹⁰N	A	T	I	V	E		¹¹	¹²A		¹³	
		I			C		¹⁴P				
¹⁵		O			O			P			
		N			N			L		¹⁶F	
		¹⁷D		¹⁸D	¹⁹E	C	I	M	A	L	
²⁰			E				C			O	
			L		²¹F	I	N	A	L	A	
²²S	O	L	I	D			T		²³X	T	
			M	²⁴			I			I	
²⁵D	I	G	I	T			O			N	
			T	²⁶			N			G	
²⁷											

© Peter Collin Publishing Ltd
Based on the *Dictionary of Computing, second edition.* ISBN 0-948549-44-0

Communicative Crossword 4   Sheet A

THIS CROSSWORD IS not complete: you have only half the words. The other half are on sheet B. Check that you know the words in your crossword. Then work with a partner who has sheet B to complete the two crosswords. Follow these three rules:

1. Speak only in English

2. Don't say the word in the crossword

3. Don't show your crossword to your partner.

> *"What's one across?"*
> → across, ↓ down

¹H		²						³P		⁴
I			■	■	■	■	■	L	■	
⁵G	L	I	T	⁶C	H	■		U	■	
H	■		■	O	■	⁷S	I	G	⁸N	A	L
D	■		■	N	■		■		U	
⁹E				T					L	
N	■			I	■		■		L	■
¹⁰S	E	¹¹T		N	■	¹²			C	
I	■		■	U	■		■		H	
¹³T				E			■		A	
Y	■		■		¹⁴				R	■
S	■		■	¹⁵U					A	■	¹⁶
¹⁷T	R	A	N	S	F	E	¹⁸R		¹⁹C	A	D
O	■		■	E	■			■	T	■
R	■			²⁰M	O	U	S	E	
²¹A					■			²²R	
G	■		■	■			■		■
E	■	²³N	E	T	W	O	R	K	I	N	G

© Peter Collin Publishing Ltd
Based on the *Dictionary of Computing, second edition.* ISBN 0-948549-44-0

Communicative Crossword 4   Sheet B

THIS CROSSWORD IS not complete: you have only half the words. The other half are on sheet A. Check that you know the words in your crossword. Then work with a partner who has sheet A to complete the two crosswords. Follow these three rules:

1. Speak only in English

2. Don't say the word in the crossword

3. Don't show your crossword to your partner.

> *"What's one across?"*
> → across, ↓ down

¹H	O	²U	S	E	K	E	E	³P	I	N	G
	■	N	■	■	■	■	■		■	■	O
⁵		I		⁶		■	■		■	■	A
	■	Q	■		■	⁷S		⁸		■	L
	■	U			■	P	■	■	■	■	■
⁹E	L	E	C	T	R	I	C	A	L	L	Y
	■	■	■		■	L	■	■		■	■
¹⁰		¹¹T				¹²L	A	T	C	H	
	■	R			■	A	■	■		■	■
¹³T	R	A	C	E	■	G	■			■	■
	■	N	■	¹⁴M	E	M	O	R	Y	■	
	■	S	■	¹⁵	■	■	■		■	¹⁶E	
¹⁷		A				¹⁸R	■	¹⁹		D	
	■	C	■		■	O	■	■	■	I	
	■	T	■	²⁰		U	■	■	■	T	
²¹A	L	I	G	N	■	T	■	²²R	S	I	
	■	O	■	■	■	E	■	■	■	N	
	■	²³N				R			■	G	

© Peter Collin Publishing Ltd
Based on the *Dictionary of Computing, second edition*. ISBN 0-948549-44-0

Communicative Crossword 5   Sheet A

THIS CROSSWORD IS not complete: you have only half the words. The other half are on sheet B. Check that you know the words in your crossword. Then work with a partner who has sheet B to complete the two crosswords. Follow these three rules:

1. Speak only in English

2. Don't say the word in the crossword

3. Don't show your crossword to your partner.

> *"What's one across?"*
> → across, ↓ down

© Peter Collin Publishing Ltd
Based on the *Dictionary of Computing, second edition.* ISBN 0-948549-44-0

Communicative Crossword 5 Sheet B

THIS CROSSWORD IS not complete: you have only half the words. The other half are on sheet A Check that you know the words in your crossword. Then work with a partner who has sheet A to complete the two crosswords. Follow these three rules:

1. Speak only in English

2. Don't say the word in the crossword

3. Don't show your crossword to your partner.

> *"What's one across?"*
> → across, ↓ down

¹S	O	²F	T	W	³A	R	⁴E	■	⁵A	■	⁶T
Y	■	I	■	■	I	■	⁷L	A	S	E	R
M	■	⁸B	A	⁹U	D	■	I	■	S	■	A
¹⁰B	A	R	■		■	■	M	■	I	■	N
O	■	¹¹E				■	I	■	G	■	S
L	■	O	■	L	■	■	N	■	N	■	A
■	■	P	U	L	L	■	¹³A	B	S	■	C
¹⁴H	O	T	■		■	■	T	■	■	¹⁵I	T
I	■	I	■	¹⁶			E		¹⁷	■	I
D	■	C	■		■	■	■	■		■	O
D	■	¹⁸S				¹⁹		■		■	N
E	■		■		■		■	■		■	■
²⁰N		²¹			■		■	■	²²S	E	²³T
■	■		■		■			■		■	A
²⁵	■		■		■		■	²⁶			G
²⁷							■	■	■	■	■
	■	■	■		■	■	²⁸		■	■	■
²⁹						■	■	³⁰			■

© Peter Collin Publishing Ltd
Based on the *Dictionary of Computing, second edition.* ISBN 0-948549-44-0

Vocabulary Record Sheet

WORD	CLASS	NOTES Translation or definition, example...

Based on the *Dictionary of Computing, second edition*. ISBN 0-948549-44-0